Pope Francis

HIS ESSENTIAL WISDOM

EDITED BY
CAROL KELLY-GANGI

FALL RIVER PRESS
New York

To John Christopher and Emily Grace with eternal love.

FALL RIVER PRESS

New York

An Imprint of Sterling Publishing
1166 Avenue of the Americas
New York, NY 10036

Jacket and book design by Scott Russo

ISBN 978-1-4351-5511-4

For information about custom editions, special sales, and premium and corporate purchases, please contact Sterling Special Sales at 800-805-5489 or specialsales@sterlingpublishing.com.

Manufactured in the United States of America

2 4 6 8 10 9 7 5 3

www.sterlingpublishing.com

CONTENTS

INTRODUCTION

"Faith does not dwell in shadow and gloom;
it is a light for our darkness."
—Pope Francis, *The Church of Mercy*

On March 13, 2013, Jorge Mario Bergoglio was elected by the College of Cardinals to become the 266th pope of the Catholic church and the leader of the 1.2 billion Catholics around the world. In just the first year of his tenure, Pope Francis has repeatedly challenged people both in and out of the church to focus on the themes of love and forgiveness that Jesus preached. With his words, gestures, and actions, Pope Francis continually reminds people about God's infinite mercy, their obligations to those in need, the meaning of humility, and the saving power of Jesus' love.

Pope Francis is the first pontiff to adopt the name of Francis. It is in the spirit of St. Francis that humility, service, and a close connection to everyday people are marking his papacy. He has garnered worldwide attention for his pastoral approach, his ardent faith, and his focus on those in need—be it the materially or the spiritually needy. He has also chosen to bypass the luxuries of his office and has instead favored a pared-down approach to daily papal living. He has opted for wearing simple shoes and vestments, residing in a Vatican guesthouse, and tooling around in a Ford Focus. People are likewise amazed at what has been dubbed by the media as his "cold calls," wherein he personally telephones someone in need to bestow comfort or offer advice. But to those who know him, these things come as no surprise. As he himself says, he is a normal person.

Pope Francis: His Essential Wisdom invites readers to experience the words of this beloved pontiff. The excerpts are drawn from his homilies, books, interviews, speeches, and other statements and writings both from his papacy and his tenure as bishop, archbishop, and cardinal. His words reveal a man who is humble, gentle, deeply spiritual, and filled with the love and mercy of God.

In the chosen excerpts, Pope Francis speaks joyfully about the eternal love of God; he invites us to open ourselves to God through prayer; he challenges us to reach out to those in need; and he reminds us of the mercy and compassion of Jesus. There are also a selection of more personal quotations, where Pope Francis recounts his calling to the priesthood and how his faith has sustained him through life's challenges. Finally, there is a selection of quotations from others about Pope Francis—from those who are well acquainted with the pope, to leaders, writers, and people from all walks of life who have been touched in some way by him.

Whether you are seeking guidance in your own spiritual journey, or want to learn more about the new pontiff who is living the Gospel and transforming lives, I hope that the words of Pope Francis, both simple and profound, will fill your heart and touch your soul.

—Carol Kelly-Gangi
New Jersey, 2014

A CALL TO SERVE

Religious vocation is a call from God to your heart, whether you are waiting for it consciously or unconsciously.

—***Pope Francis: Conversations with Jorge Bergoglio***
edited by Francesca Ambrogetti and Sergio Rubin

During that confession something unusual happened to me. I cannot say what, but it was something that changed my life. I would say that it was as though I had been surprised while my guard was down. It was the surprise, the amazement of an encounter for which I realized I had been waiting. This is the religious experience: the amazement of meeting someone who is expecting you.

—***Francis: Pope of a New World*** **by Andrea Tornielli,**
translated by William J. Melcher

I told my father first, and he took it very well. More than well: he was happy. The only thing he did was ask me if I was absolutely certain about my decision. He later told my mother, who, being a good mother, already had an inkling.

—***Pope Francis: Conversations with Jorge Bergoglio***
edited by Francesca Ambrogetti and Sergio Rubin

Please do not forget to pray for me, since I do need it.

—Homily, July 29, 2007

I entered the diocesan seminary. I liked the Dominicans, and I had Dominican friends. But then I chose the Society of Jesus, which I knew well because the seminary was entrusted to the Jesuits. Three things in particular struck me about the Society: the missionary spirit, community and discipline.

—Interview with Antonio Spadaro, S.J., editor-in-chief of *La Civiltà Cattolica*, August–September 2013

Do not be afraid to go and to bring Christ into every area of life, to the fringes of society, even to those who seem farthest away, most indifferent.

—World Youth Day Mass, July 28, 2013

Yesterday I celebrated the 60th anniversary of the day when I heard Jesus' voice in my heart. . . . I will never forget it. The Lord made me strongly aware that I should take that path. . . . No, I have not regretted it because always, even at the darkest moments, the moments of sin and moments of frailty, moments of failure, I have looked at Jesus and trusted in him, and he has not deserted me. Trust in Jesus: he always keeps on going, he goes with us!

—Address to young people, Calgiari, Sardinia September 22, 2013

When I pray for the city of Buenos Aires, I am grateful for the fact that I was born in this city. The love that flows from such familiarity helps me to embody the universality of faith that embraces all men and women of every city.

—Opening remarks at the First Regional Congress of Urban Ministry in Buenos Aires, August 25, 2011

I want things messy and stirred up in the congregations. I want you to take to the streets. I want the church to take to the streets.

—Address at the Cathedral of San Sebastian, July 25, 2013

POPE FRANCIS

Before I accepted, I asked if I could spend a few minutes in the room next to the one with the balcony overlooking the square. My head was completely empty and I was seized by a great anxiety. . . . I closed my eyes and I no longer had any anxiety or emotion. At a certain point I was filled with a great light. It lasted a moment, but to me it seemed very long. Then the light faded, I got up suddenly and walked into the room where the cardinals were waiting and the table on which was the act of acceptance.

—Interview with *La Repubblica* founder, Eugenio Scalfari, October 1, 2013

Brothers and sisters, good evening! You know that it was the duty of the conclave to give Rome a bishop. It seems that my brother cardinals have gone to the ends of the earth to get one. . . but here we are. . . . And now, we take up this journey: bishop and people. This journey of the Church of Rome which presides in charity over all the Churches. A journey of fraternity, of love, of trust among us. Let us always pray for one another. Let us pray for the whole world, that there may be a great spirit of fraternity. . . . And now I would like to give the blessing, but first—first I ask a favor of you: before the bishop blesses his people, I ask you to pray to the Lord that he will bless me: the prayer of the people asking the blessing for their bishop. Let us make, in silence, this prayer: your prayer over me.

— Pope Francis's first blessing and message to Rome and the world, delivered from the balcony of St. Peter's Basilica, March 13, 2013

Thank you for all your warm wishes on my anniversary. Please continue praying for me.

—Tweet, March 17, 2014

I am going on the bus because I came here on the bus with all of you. I will go back on the bus.

—Pope Francis declines the papal limo after his election. He instead takes a shuttle bus with the other cardinals back to Casa Santa Marta, March 13, 2013

During the election, I was seated next to the Archbishop Emeritus of São Paolo . . . a good friend. . . . And when the votes reached two thirds, there was the usual applause, because the Pope had been elected. And he gave me a hug and a kiss, and said: "Don't forget the poor!" And those words came to me: the poor, the poor. Then, right away, thinking of the poor, I thought of Francis of Assisi. Then I thought of all the wars, as the votes were still being counted, till the end. Francis is also the man of peace. That is how the name came into my heart: Francis of Assisi.

—Pope Francis on the choosing of his name, Vatican press conference, March 16, 2013

For me, his is the man of poverty, the man of peace, the man who loves and protects creation; these days we do not have a very good relationship with creation, do we? He is the man who gives us this spirit of peace, the poor man. . . . How I would like a Church which is poor and for the poor!

—Vatican press conference, March 16, 2013

My wish is that all of us, after these days of grace, will have the courage, yes, the courage, to walk in the presence of the Lord, with the Lord's Cross; to build the Church on the Lord's blood which was poured out on the Cross; and to profess the one glory: Christ crucified. And in this way, the Church will go forward. My prayer for all of us is that the Holy Spirit, through the intercession of the Blessed Virgin Mary, our Mother, will grant us this grace: to walk, to build, to profess Jesus Christ crucified. Amen.

—Mass with cardinal electors, March 14, 2013

Let us never forget that authentic power is service, and that the Pope too, when exercising power, must enter ever more fully into that service which has its radiant culmination in the Cross. He must be inspired by the lowly, concrete and faithful service which marked Saint Joseph and, like him, he must open his arms to protect all of God's people and embrace with tender affection the whole humanity, especially the poorest, the weakest, the least important . . .

—Homily, inaugural Mass, March 19, 2013

This is me, a sinner on whom the Lord has turned his gaze. And this is what I said when they asked me if I would accept my election as pontiff. I am a sinner, but I trust in the infinite mercy and patience of our Lord Jesus Christ, and I accept in a spirit of penance.

—Interview with Antonio Spadaro, S.J., editor-in-chief of *La Civiltà Cattolica*, August–September 2013

Christ is the Church's Pastor, but his presence in history passes through the freedom of human beings; from their midst one is chosen to serve as his Vicar, the Successor of the Apostle Peter.

—Vatican press conference, March 16, 2013

But I am the Bishop of Rome and Pope of the Catholic world. The first thing I decided was to appoint a group of eight cardinals to be my advisers. Not courtiers but wise people who share my own feelings. This is the beginning of a Church with an organization that is not just top-down but also horizontal.

—Interview with *La Repubblica* founder, Eugenio Scalfari, October 1, 2013

To depict the pope as a sort of superman, a sort of star, seems offensive to me. The pope is a man who laughs, cries, sleeps tranquilly and has friends like everyone else, a normal person.

—Interview, *Corriere della Sera*, March 2014

Help one another: This is what Jesus teaches us, and this is what I am doing—and doing with all my heart—because it is my duty. As a priest and a bishop, I must be at your service. But is a duty that comes from my heart. I love it.

—Homily, Holy Thursday, March 28, 2013

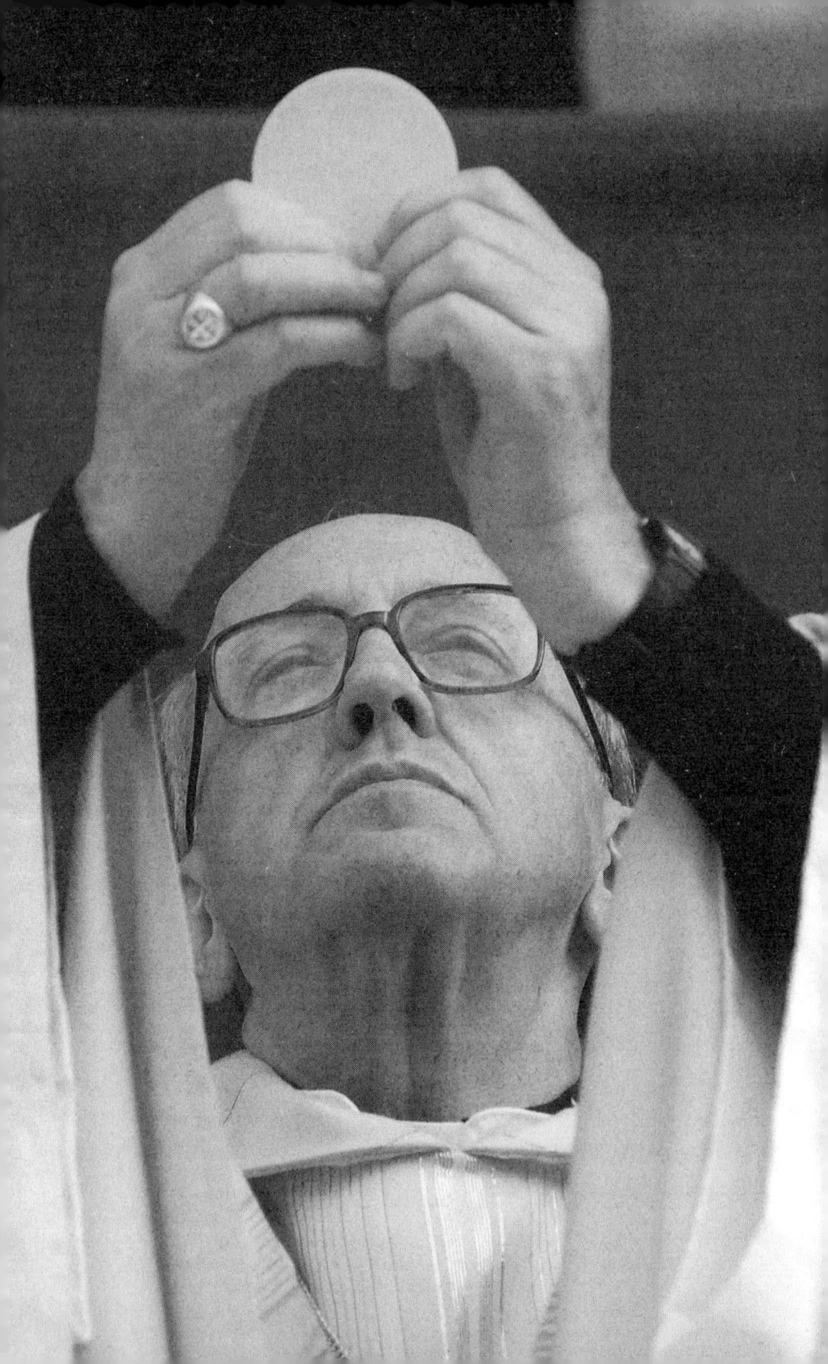

GOD THE FATHER, THE SON, AND THE HOLY SPIRIT

God does not wait for us to go to him, but it is he who moves toward us, without calculation, without quantification. That is what God is like. He always takes the first step; he comes toward us.

—Pope Francis's first general audience, March 27, 2013

God makes Himself felt in the heart of each person. He also respects the culture of all people. Each nation picks up that vision of God and translates it in accordance with the culture, and elaborates, purifies and gives it a system. Some cultures are primitive in their explanations, but God is open to all people. He calls everyone. He moves everyone to seek Him and to discover Him through creation.

—On Heaven and Earth: Pope Francis on Faith, Family, and the Church in the Twenty-First Century
by Jorge Mario Bergoglio and Abraham Skorka

God thinks like the Samaritan who did not pass by the unfortunate man, pitying him or looking at him from the other side of the road, but helped him without asking for anything in return; without asking whether he was a Jew, a pagan or a Samaritan, whether he was rich or poor: he asked for nothing. He went to help him: God is like this.

—General audience, March 27, 2013

The Sacraments, especially Confession and the Eucharist, are privileged places of encountering Christ.

—Tweet, February 8, 2014

And I believe in God, not in a Catholic God, there is no Catholic God, there is God and I believe in Jesus Christ, his incarnation. Jesus is my teacher and my pastor, but God, the Father, Abba, is the light and the Creator. This is my Being.

—Interview with *La Repubblica* founder, Eugenio Scalfari, October 1, 2013

"God is love." His is not a sentimental, emotional kind of love but the love of the Father who is the origin of all life, the love of the Son who dies on the cross and is raised, the love of the Spirit who renews human beings and the world. Thinking that God is love does us so much good, because it teaches us to love, to give ourselves to others as Jesus gave himself to us and walks with us. Jesus walks beside us on the road through life.

—Angelus address, May 26, 2013

Let us remember this: God judges us by loving us. If I embrace his love, then I am saved; if I refuse it, then I am condemned, not by him, but my own self, because God never condemns; he only loves and saves.

—Address, World Youth Day, July 26, 2013

Jesus is our hope. Nothing—not even evil or death—is able to separate us from the saving power of his love.

—Tweet, March 22, 2014

Jesus is the incarnation of the Living God, the one who brings life amid so many deeds of death, amid sin, selfishness, and self-absorption. Jesus accepts, loves, uplifts, encourages, forgives, restores the ability to walk, gives back life.

—Homily, June 16, 2013

Jesus is called the Lamb: He is the Lamb who takes away the sin of the world. Someone might think: but how can a lamb, which is so weak, a weak little lamb, how can it take away so many sins, so much wickedness? With Love. With his meekness. Jesus never ceased being a lamb: meek, good, full of love, close to the little ones, close to the poor. He was there, among the people, healing everyone, teaching, praying. Jesus, so weak, like a lamb. However, he had the strength to take all our sins upon himself, all of them.

—Homily, January 19, 2014

What is the most important thing? Jesus. If we forge ahead with our own arrangements, with other things, with beautiful things but without Jesus, we make no headway, it does not work. Jesus is more important.

—Address, Pentecost vigil with ecclesial movements, May 18, 2013

He who encounters Jesus Christ feels the impulse to witness him or to give witness of what he has encountered, and this is the Christian calling.

—Lecture, 2001

What does it mean that Jesus is risen? It means that the love of God is stronger than evil and death itself; it means that the love of God can transform our lives and let those desert places in our hearts bloom. The love of God can do this!

—Easter Sunday message, March 31, 2013

Ask yourselves this question: How often is Jesus inside and knocking at the door to be let out, to come out? And we do not let him out because of our own need for security, because so often we are locked into ephemeral structures that serve solely to make us slaves and not free children of God.

—Address, Pentecost vigil with ecclesial movements, May 18, 2013

A revolution, in order to transform history, must profoundly change human hearts. Revolutions that have taken place throughout the centuries have changed political and economic systems, but none of them have truly changed the human heart. Only Jesus Christ accomplished the true revolution, the one that radically transforms life, with his Resurrection that, as Benedict XVI loves to recall, was "the greatest 'mutation' in the history of humanity" and it gave birth to a new world.

—Address to Ecclesial Convention of Rome, June 17, 2013

I think we too are the people who, on the one hand, want to listen to Jesus, but on the other hand, at times, like to find a stick to beat others with, to condemn others. And Jesus has this message for us: mercy. I think—and I say it with humility—that this is the Lord's most powerful message: mercy.

—Homily, March 17, 2013

Why the Cross? Because Jesus takes upon himself the evil, the filth, the sin of the world, including the sin of all of us, and he cleanses it, he cleanses it with his blood, with the mercy and the love of God. . . . Jesus on the Cross feels the whole weight of the evil, and with the force of God's love he conquers it, he defeats it with his resurrection.

—Homily, Palm Sunday and World Youth Day, March 24, 2013

Following and accompanying Christ, staying with him, demands "coming out of ourselves" . . . out of a dreary way of living faith that has become a habit, out of the temptation to withdraw into our own plans which end by shutting out God's creative action.

—General audience, March 27, 2013

Christ is the fundamental point of reference, the heart of the Church. Without him, Peter and the Church would not exist or have reason to exist.

—Vatican press conference, March 16, 2013

The Holy Spirit would appear to create disorder in the Church, since he brings the diversity of charisms and gifts; yet all this, by his working, is a great source of wealth, for the Holy Spirit is the Spirit of unity, which does not mean uniformity, but which leads everything back to harmony.

—Homily, Pentecost, May 19, 2013

The Holy Spirit is the soul of the Church, with His life-giving and unifying strength. Of many He makes a single body—the mystical Body of Christ.

—Address to the cardinals, March 15, 2013

It is the Paraclete Spirit, the "Comforter," who grants us the courage to take to the streets of the world, bringing the Gospel! The Holy Spirit makes us look to the horizon and drives us to the very outskirts of existence in order to proclaim life in Jesus Christ. Let us ask ourselves: do we tend to stay closed in on ourselves, on our group, or do we let the Holy Spirit open us to mission?

—Homily, Pentecost, May 19, 2013

LOVE

Love is the greatest power for the transformation of reality because it pulls down the walls of selfishness and fills the ditches that keep us apart. This is the love that comes from a mutated heart, from a heart of stone that has been turned into a heart of flesh, a human heart.

—Angelus address, June 17, 2013

I am thinking of what St Ignatius told us . . . He pointed out two criteria on love. The first: love is expressed more clearly in actions than in words. The second: there is greater love in giving than in receiving.

—Morning meditation, Friday June 7, 2013

Love shares everything it has and reveals itself in communication. There is no true faith that is not manifested in love. And love is not Christian love if it is not generous and concrete. A decidedly generous love is a sign of faith and an invitation to faith. When we care for the needs of our brothers and sisters, like the Good Samaritan did, we are proclaiming the Kingdom and making it present.

—Lenten letter from Cardinal Bergoglio, February 22, 2012

You tell us that to love God and neighbor is not something abstract, but profoundly concrete: it means seeing in every person the face of the Lord to be served, to serve him concretely. And you are, dear brothers and sisters, the face of Jesus.

—Address during visit to homeless shelter, May 21, 2013

The worst thing that can happen to us is to be without love, so as to look out only for our self-interest. Mary is the woman of love. Without love, there is no room for life. Without love there is selfishness and one turns in on oneself so as to coddle oneself. Today we ask Mary for love so as to care for life. Love and courage!

—Homily, May 25, 2012

We already know where the voracious greed for power, the imposition of one's ideas as absolute, and the rejection of those who think differently will take us: to a numbness of conscience and to abandonment. Only the commitment of love in all its simplicity—steady, humble, unassuming but firm in conviction and in commitment to others—can save us.

—Homily, May 25, 2012

Establishing love is a work of skillful craftsmanship, the work of patient people, people who do their utmost to persuade, to listen, to bring people together. This skillful work is carried out peacefully and wonderfully by creators of love. It is the task of the mediator. . . . A mediator is a person who, in order to bring two sides together, personally pays the price to do so. He wears himself out in the process.

—Homily, September 6, 2008

We have observed that, in society and the world in which we live, selfishness has increased more than love for others, and that men of good will must work, each with his own strengths and expertise, to ensure that love for others increases until it is equal and possibly exceeds love for oneself.

—Interview with *La Repubblica* founder, Eugenio Scalfari, October 1, 2013

God's becoming man is a great mystery! But the reason for all this is His love, a love which is grace, generosity, a desire to draw near, a love which does not hesitate to offer itself in sacrifice for the beloved. Charity, love, is sharing with the one we love in all things. Love makes us similar, it creates equality, it breaks down walls and eliminates distances. God did this with us.

—Lenten message, 2014

Jesus wants to love you for what you are, even in your frailty and weakness, so that moved by his love, you may be renewed.

—Message, June 21, 2013

"But Father, I don't know how to love." No one knows how to love; we learn every day.

—Homily, April 21, 2004

If we are truly in love with Christ and if we sense how much he loves us, our heart will "light up" with a joy that spreads to everyone around us.

—Homily, Mass in the Basilica of the Shrine of Our Lady of the Conception, Aparecida, Brazil, July 24, 2013

Whenever we encounter another person in love, we learn something new about God.

***—The Joy of the Gospel: Apostolic Exhortation*, 2013**

HUMILITY AND SIMPLICITY

Christian humility is not within the virtue of saying: "I am not important" and hiding our pride. No, Christian humility is telling the truth: "I am a sinner."

—Homily, March 24, 2014

Humility reveals, to the smallness of our human self-awareness, its power. In effect, however, when we are more conscious of both our gifts and limitations, we will be more free of the blindness of pride.

—Homily, March 15, 2013

Some will say: joy is born from possessions . . . but I tell you, it truly grieves me to see a priest or a sister with the latest model of a car. . . . I think that cars are necessary because there is so much work to be done, and also in order to get about . . . but choose a more humble car! And if you like the beautiful one, only think of all the children who are dying of hunger.

—Address to seminarians and novices, July 6, 2013

But what kind of a king is Jesus? Let us take a look at him: he is riding on a donkey, he is not accompanied by a court, he is not surrounded by an army as a symbol of power. He is received by humble people, simple folk who have the sense to see something more in Jesus.

—Homily, Palm Sunday and World Youth Day, March 24, 2013

Benedict XVI, with great wisdom, often reminded the Church that although man frequently equates authority with control, dominion, success, for God authority is always synonymous with service, humility, love; it means entering the logic of Jesus, who kneels to wash the apostles' feet.

—Address, May 8, 2013

My choices, including those related to the day-to-day aspects of life, like the use of a modest car, are related to a spiritual discernment that responds to a need that arises from looking at things, at people and from reading the signs of the times. Discernment in the Lord guides me in my way of governing.

—Interview with Antonio Spadaro, S.J., editor-in-chief of *La Civiltà Cattolica*, August–September 2013

This is humility, the path of humility: to feel so marginalized that we need the Salvation of the Lord. He alone saves us, not our observance of the law.

—Homily, March 24, 2014

The Jesus who was weak and insignificant in the eyes of politicians and the powerful of the land revolutionized the world.

—Homily, May 25, 2012

Real power is found in service. Just like Jesus, who didn't come to be served but to serve. His service was seen on the Cross. He humbled Himself unto death, He died on a Cross for us, to serve us, to save us. It's with this path that the Church moves forward. For the Christian, getting ahead, progress, means humbling oneself. If we do not learn this Christian rule, we will never, ever be able to understand Jesus' true message on power.

—Homily, May 21, 2013

If they are hungry, mothers, feed them, without thinking twice. Because they are the most important people here.

—Pope Francis's advising mothers at a baptism in the Sistine Chapel to feel free to breast-feed their babies there, January 12, 2014

He will not find us at the center of our certainties. That is not where the Lord looks. He will find us on the margins, in our sins, in our mistakes, in our need for spiritual healing, for salvation; that is where the Lord will find us.

—Homily, March 24, 2014

A simple lifestyle is good for us, helping us to better share with those in need.

—Tweet, April 24, 2014

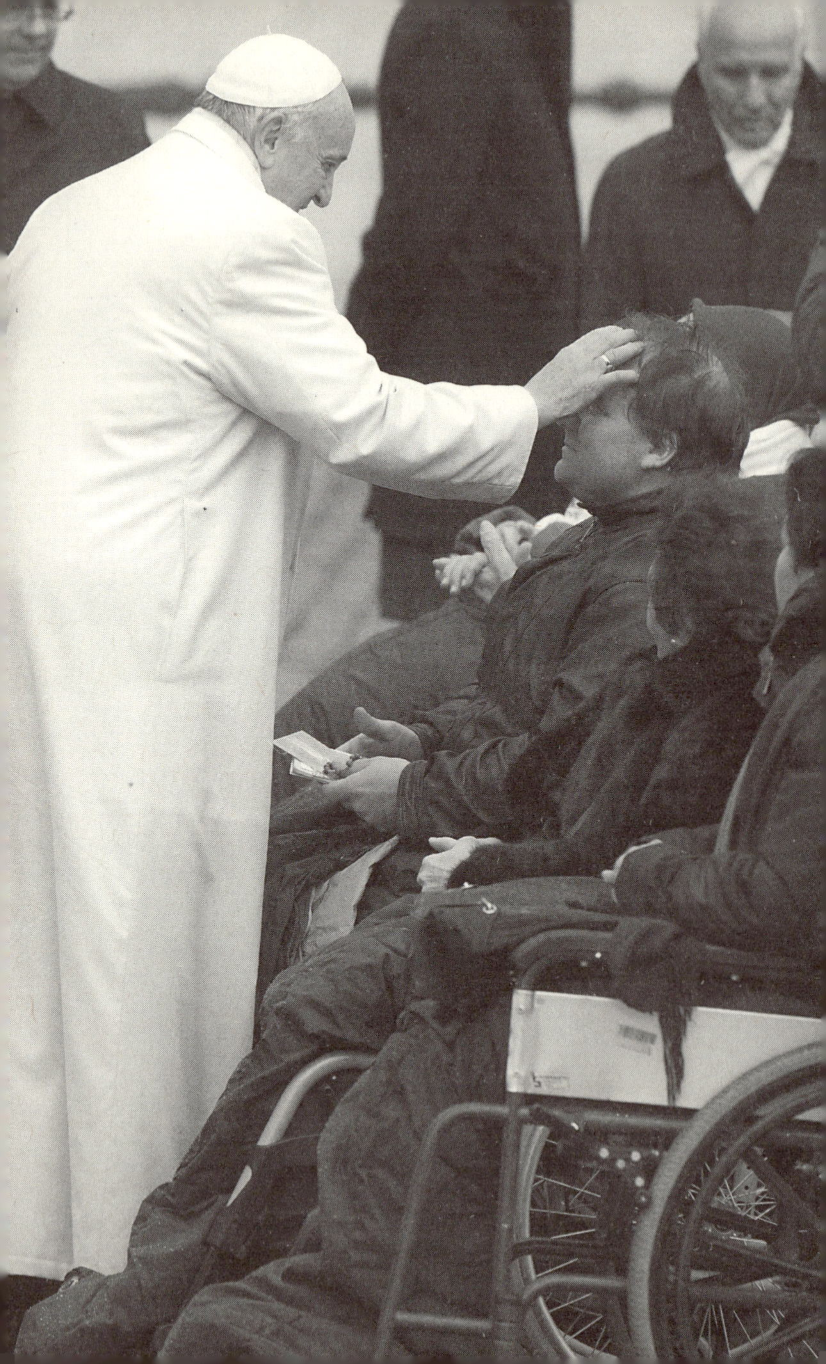

PRAYER, FAITH, AND HOPE

Miracles happen. But prayer is needed! Prayer that is courageous, struggling, and persevering, not prayer that is a mere formality.

—Tweet, May 24, 2013

It is easy to ask God for things; we all do it. When will we also learn to give him thanks and to adore him?

—Tweet, January 25, 2014

If we look toward Jesus, we see that prior to any important decision or event he recollected himself in intense and prolonged prayer. Let us cultivate the contemplative dimension, even amid the whirlwind of more urgent and heavy duties. And the more the mission calls you to go out to the margins of existence, let your heart be the more closely united to Christ's heart, full of mercy and love.

—Homily, Mass with seminarians and novices, July 7, 2013

This is a prayer we must pray every day: "Holy Spirit, make my heart open to the word of God, make my heart open to goodness, make my heart open to the beauty of God every day." I would like to ask everyone a question: How many of you pray every day to the Holy Spirit? There will not be many but we must fulfill Jesus' wish and pray every day to the Holy Spirit that he open our heart to Jesus.

—Homily, May 15, 2013

And in this month of May, I would like to recall the importance and beauty of the prayer of the Holy Rosary. Reciting the Hail Mary, we are led to contemplate the mysteries of Jesus, that is, to reflect on the key moments of his life, so that, as with Mary and St. Joseph, he is the center of our thoughts, of our attention and our actions.

—Homily, May 1, 2013

In our Christian life too, dear brothers and sisters, may prayer and action always be deeply united. A prayer that does not lead you to practical action for your brother—the poor, the sick, those in need of help, a brother in difficulty—is a sterile and incomplete prayer. But, in the same way, when ecclesial service is attentive only to doing, things gain in importance, functions, structures, and we forget the centrality of Christ. When time is not set aside for dialogue with him in prayer, we risk serving ourselves and not God present in our needy brother and sister.

—Angelus address, July 21, 2013

Faith is not a light which scatters all our darkness, but a lamp which guides our steps in the night and suffices for the journey. To those who suffer, God does not provide arguments which explain everything; rather, his response is that of an accompanying presence, a history of goodness which touches every story of suffering and opens up a ray of light.

—*Lumen Fidei*, 2013

Faith means choosing God as the criterion and basis of life—and God is not empty, God is not neutral, God is always positive, God is love, and love is positive!

—Angelus address, August 11, 2013

We must not let ourselves fall into the vortex of pessimism. Faith can move mountains!

—Tweet, April 25, 2014

Faith is no refuge for the fainthearted, but something which enhances our lives. It makes us aware of a magnificent calling, the vocation of love. It assures us that this love is trustworthy and worth embracing, for it is based on God's faithfulness, which is stronger than our every weakness.

—*Lumen Fidei*, 2013

Let us all remember this: one cannot proclaim the Gospel of Jesus without the tangible witness of one's life. Those who listen to us and observe us must be able to see in our actions what they hear from our lips, and so give glory to God! I am thinking now of some advice that Saint Francis of Assisi gave his brothers: preach the Gospel and, if necessary, use words. [Preach] with your life, with your witness.

—Homily, April 14, 2013

Prayer always reaches God, as long as it is prayer from the heart.

—Homily, June 5, 2013

Do not be afraid to live out faith! Be witnesses of Christ in your daily environment, with simplicity and courage. Above all, may you be able to show those you meet, your peers, the Face of mercy and the love of God who always forgives, encourages, and imbues hope.

—Message, June 21, 2013

How many sad people, how many sad people without hope! . . . They have tried so many things and society, which is cruel—it is cruel!—it cannot give you hope. Hope is like grace: it cannot be bought, it is a gift of God. We must offer Christian hope with our witness, our freedom and our joy. The present offered by the God of grace gives hope.

—Address to Ecclesial Convention of the Diocese of Rome, June 17, 2013

It's best to not confuse optimism with hope. Optimism is a psychological attitude toward life. Hope goes further. It is an anchor that one hurls toward the future, it's what lets you pull on the line and reach what you're aiming for. . . .

—*El Jesuita*, 2010

In the authenticity of our hope we know how to discover, in daily life, the great or small reasons to recognize the gifts of God, to celebrate life, to emerge from the chain of "ought" and "have to" so as to unfold the joy of beings seeds of a new creation.

—*Inspiration from Pope Francis* compiled by Maria Gabriela Flores, FSP

To protect creation, to protect every man and every woman, to look upon them with tenderness and love, is to open up a horizon of hope; it is to let a shaft of light break through the heavy clouds; it is to bring the warmth of hope!

—Homily, inaugural Mass, March 19, 2013

Let us follow Jesus! We accompany, we follow Jesus, but above all we know that he accompanies us and carries us on his shoulders. This is our joy, this is the hope that we must bring to this world. Please do not let yourselves be robbed of hope! Do not let hope be stolen! The hope that Jesus gives us!

—Homily, Palm Sunday and World Youth Day, March 24, 2013

SERVING GOD

You, are you brave enough for this, do you have the courage to hear the voice of Jesus? It is beautiful to be missionaries! . . . Everyone must be a missionary, everyone can hear that call of Jesus and go forth and proclaim the Kingdom!

—Angelus address, July 7, 2013

This gesture is an invitation to the heart of every Christian, because we never lose if we imitate Jesus, if we . . . serve our suffering brothers.

—Pope Francis on washing the feet of AIDS patients, as reported in the *Wall Street Journal*, March 14, 2013

Dear brothers and sisters, the Church loves you! Be an active presence in the community, as living cells, as living stones.

—Homily, May 5, 2013

The Gospel is for everyone! This reaching out to the poor does not mean we must become champions of poverty or, as it were, "spiritual tramps"! No, no this is not what it means! It means we must reach out to the flesh of Jesus that is suffering, but also suffering is the flesh of Jesus of those who do not know it with their study, with their intelligence, with their culture. We must go there!

—Address to Ecclesial Convention of the Diocese of Rome, June 17, 2013

Those who have opened their hearts to God's love, heard his voice, and received his light cannot keep this gift to themselves. Since faith is hearing and seeing, it is also handed on as word and light.

—*Lumen Fidei*, 2013

Let us ask ourselves: how do I follow Jesus? Jesus speaks in silence in the Mystery of the Eucharist. He reminds us every time that following him means going out of ourselves and not making our life a possession of our own, but rather a gift to him and to others.

—Homily, May 30, 2013

One of the more serious temptations which stifles boldness and zeal is a defeatism which turns us into querulous and disillusioned pessimists, sourpusses.

—*The Joy of the Gospel: Apostolic Exhortation*, 2013

An evangelizer must never look like someone who has just come back from a funeral.

—*The Joy of the Gospel: Apostolic Exhortation*, 2013

In the Gospel there's that beautiful passage that tells us of the shepherd who, on returning to the sheepfold and realizing that a sheep is missing, leaves the 99 and goes to look for . . . the one. But, brothers and sisters, we have one. It's the 99 who we're missing! We have to go out. . . . we must ask the Lord for the grace of generosity and the courage and the patience to go out, to go out and proclaim the Gospel.

This is precisely the reason for the dissatisfaction of some, who end up sad—sad priests—in some sense becoming collectors of antiques or novelties, instead of being shepherds living with "the odor of the sheep." This I ask you: Be shepherds, with the "odor of the sheep," make it real, as shepherds among your flock, fishers of men.

—Homily, March 28, 2013

In our ecclesiastical region, there are priests who don't baptize the children of single mothers because they weren't conceived in the sanctity of marriage. These are today's hypocrites. Those who clericalize the Church. Those who separate the people of God from salvation. And this poor girl who, rather than returning the child to sender, had the courage to carry it into the world, must wander from parish to parish so that it's baptized!

—Homily, September 2, 2012

To be an open priest is to be capable of listening while remaining firm in one's convictions.

—Letter to the priests of the archdiocese, October 1, 1999

I usually tell priests that when they are in the confessional, they should be neither too severe nor excessively indulgent. The disciplinarian is one who applies the rules without a second thought. "The law says this, and that's that," he says. The lenient one sweeps it aside. "It's fine, whatever, life is like that, move on," he says. . . . "And so, Father, what should we do?" they ask me. And I tell them, "Be compassionate."

—*Pope Francis: Conversations with Jorge Bergoglio*
edited by Francesca Ambrogetti and Sergio Rubin

A good priest can be recognized by the way his people are anointed: this is a clear proof. When our people are anointed with the oil of gladness, it is obvious: for example, when they leave Mass looking as if they have heard good news. . . . People thank us because they feel that we have prayed over the realities of their everyday lives, their troubles, their joys, their burdens and their hopes.

—Homily, March 28, 2013

Formation [of priests] is a work of art, not a police action. We must form their hearts. Otherwise we are creating little monsters. And these little monsters mold the people of God. This really gives me goosebumps.

—Address to leaders of men's religious orders meeting in Rome, November 29, 2013

We cannot become starched Christians, those over-educated Christians who speak of theological matters as they calmly sip their tea. No! We must become courageous Christians and go in search of the people who are the very flesh of Christ, those who are the flesh of Christ!

—Address, Pentecost vigil with ecclesial movements, May 18, 2013

Preparation for preaching is so important a task that a prolonged time of study, prayer, reflection and pastoral creativity should be devoted to it. . . . a preacher who does not prepare is not "spiritual"; he is dishonest and irresponsible with the gifts he has received.

—*The Joy of the Gospel: Apostolic Exhortation*, 2013

Who would claim to lock up in a church and silence the message of St. Francis of Assisi or Blessed Teresa of Calcutta? They themselves would have found this unacceptable. An authentic faith—which is never comfortable or completely personal—always involves a deep desire to change the world, to transmit values, to leave this earth somehow better than we found it.

—*The Joy of the Gospel: Apostolic Exhortation*, 2013

Being a disciple means being constantly ready to bring the love of Jesus to others, and this can happen unexpectedly and in any place: on the street, in a city square, during work, on a journey.

—*The Joy of the Gospel: Apostolic Exhortation*, 2013

We find Jesus' wounds in carrying out works of mercy, giving to our body—the body—the soul too, but—I stress—the body of your wounded brother, because he is hungry, because he is thirsty, because he is naked, because he is humiliated, because he is a slave, because he's in jail, because he is in the hospital. Those are the wounds of Jesus today.

—Homily, July 3, 2013

In fidelity to the Gospel, and in response to the urgent needs of the present time, we are called to reach out to those who find themselves in the existential peripheries of our societies and to show particular solidarity with the most vulnerable of our brothers and sisters: the poor, the disabled, the unborn and the sick, migrants and refugees, the elderly and the young who lack employment.

—Message to Cardinal Kurt Koch on the Occasion of the 10th General Assembly of the World Council of Churches, October 4, 2013

We must prepare ourselves for the spiritual combat. This is important. It is impossible to preach the Gospel without this spiritual battle, a daily battle against sadness, against bitterness, against pessimism; a daily battle!

—Address to Ecclesial Convention of the Diocese of Rome, June 17, 2013

The cardinalate is a service—it is not an award to be bragged about. Vanity, showing off, is an attitude that reduces spirituality to a worldly thing, which is the worst sin that could be committed in the Church. . . . An example I often use to illustrate the reality of vanity, is this: look at the peacock; it's beautiful if you look at it from the front. But if you look at it from behind, you discover the truth . . . Whoever gives in to such self-absorbed vanity has huge misery hiding inside them.

—*National Catholic Reporter*, "Francis: What is in a name?" by Thomas Reese, March 13, 2013

I am in favor of maintaining celibacy, with the pros and the cons that it has, because it has been ten centuries of good experiences more often than failures.

—*On Heaven and Earth: Pope Francis on Faith, Family, and the Church in the Twenty-First Century* by Jorge Mario Bergoglio and Abraham Skorka

Let us never give in to pessimism, to that bitterness that the devil tempts us with every day. Let us not give in to pessimism, and let us not be discouraged. We have the certainty that the Holy Spirit gives his Church, with his powerful breath, the courage to persevere, the courage to persevere and to search for new ways to evangelize, to bring the Gospel to the ends of the earth.

—Address to College of Cardinals, March 15, 2013

May you always be attentive to charity. Each individual Christian and every community is missionary to the extent that they bring to others and live the Gospel, and testify to God's love for all, especially those experiencing difficulties. Be missionaries of God's love and tenderness!

—Homily, May 5, 2013

SOCIAL JUSTICE

We are in front of a global scandal of around one billion—one billion people who still suffer from hunger today. We cannot look the other way and pretend this does not exist. The food available in the world is enough to feed everyone.

—Video message launching a campaign against hunger, December 9, 2013

It is a well-known fact that current levels of production are sufficient, yet millions of people are still suffering and dying of starvation. This, dear friends is truly scandalous. A way has to be found to enable everyone to benefit from the fruits of the earth, and not simply to close the gap between the affluent and those who must be satisfied with the crumbs falling from the table, but above all to satisfy the demands of justice, fairness and respect for every human being.

—Address to United Nations Food and Agricultural Organization Conference, June 20, 2013

Men and women are sacrificed to the idols of profit and consumption: it is the "culture of waste." If a computer breaks it is a tragedy, but poverty, the needs and dramas of so many people end up being considered normal. . . . When the stock market drops 10 points in some cities, it constitutes a tragedy. Someone who dies is not news, but lowering income by 10 points is a tragedy! In this way people are thrown aside as if they were trash.

—General audience, June 5, 2013

Some people continue to defend trickle-down theories which assume that economic growth, encouraged by a free market, will inevitably succeed in bringing about greater justice and inclusiveness in the world. This opinion, which has never been confirmed by the facts, expresses a crude and naïve trust in the goodness of those wielding economic power and in the sacralized workings of the prevailing economic system.

—*The Joy of the Gospel: Apostolic Exhortation*, 2013

I encourage the financial experts and the political leaders of your countries to consider the words of Saint John Chrysostom: "Not to share one's goods with the poor is to rob them and to deprive them of life. It is not our goods that we possess, but theirs."

—Audience with ambassadors, May 16, 2013

In this city are many human sacrifices that kill the dignity of these men and women, these boys and girls subjected to trafficking and slavery. We cannot stay quiet. This city is full of men and women, boys and girls beaten by the wayside, beaten by the organization or organizations that are corrupting, removing the will, even destroying them with drugs. And then they are left lying by the roadside.

—Homily, 2010

Just as the commandment "Thou shalt not kill" sets a clear limit in order to safeguard the value of human life, today we also have to say "thou shalt not" to an economy of exclusion and inequality. Such an economy kills. How can it be that it is not a news item when an elderly homeless person dies of exposure, but it is news when the stock market loses two points?

—***The Joy of the Gospel: Apostolic Exhortation*, 2013**

At times I have thought about all the expense that goes into taking care of a pet; it could be spent on food and education for a child who does not have these things. Do we take a concern for the lives of these children as they grow? Do we worry about the company they keep? Do we take a concern to see them grow up free and mature?

—Homily, March 25, 2011

The thirst for power and possessions knows no limits. In this system, which tends to devour everything which stands in the way of increased profits, whatever is fragile, like the environment, is defenseless before the interests of a deified market, which become the only rule.

—***The Joy of the Gospel: Apostolic Exhortation*, 2013**

In imitation of our Master, we Christians are called to confront the poverty of our brothers and sisters, to touch it, to make it our own and to take practical steps to alleviate it.

—Lenten message, 2014

Money has to serve, not rule! The pope loves everyone, rich and poor alike, but the pope has the duty, in Christ's name, to remind the rich to help the poor, to respect them, to promote them. The pope appeals for disinterested solidarity and for a return to person-centered ethics in the world of finance and economics.

—Address to nonresident ambassadors to the Holy See, May 16, 2013

Nature, in a word, is at our disposition and we are called to exercise a responsible stewardship over it. Yet so often we are driven by greed and by the arrogance of dominion, possession, manipulation and exploitation; we do not preserve nature; nor do we respect it or consider it a gracious gift which we must care for and set at the service of our brothers and sisters, including future generations.

—Message for World Day of Peace, January 1, 2014

Each day, we all face the choice to be Good Samaritans or to be indifferent travelers passing by.

—Homily, May 25, 2003

Man is not in charge today, money is in charge, money rules. God our Father did not give the task of caring for the earth to money, but to us, to men and women: we have this task! Instead, men and women are sacrificed to the idols of profit and consumption: it is the "culture of waste."

—General audience on United Nations World Environment Day, June 5, 2013

Please, I would like to ask all those who have positions of responsibility in economic, political and social life, and all men and women of goodwill: let us be "protectors" of creation, protectors of God's plan inscribed in nature, protectors of one another and of the environment.

—Homily, inaugural Mass, March 19, 2013

A society that abandons children and marginalizes the elderly severs its roots and obscures its future. Whenever a child is abandoned and an old person is marginalized, is not just an act of injustice, but it also demonstrates the failure of that society. Taking care of children and the elderly is the only choice of civilization.

—Address to XXI Plenary Assembly of the Pontifical Council for the Family, October 2013

We do not live better when we flee, hide, refuse to share, stop giving and lock ourselves up in [our] own comforts. Such a life is nothing less than slow suicide.

—*The Joy of the Gospel: Apostolic Exhortation*, 2013

FAMILY LIFE

The family is the natural center of human life.

—Address to XXI Plenary Assembly of the Pontifical Council for the Family, October 2013

In the family, a person becomes aware of his own dignity, and especially if his education is Christian, recognizes the dignity of every human person, and in a special way, that of the sick, weak and marginalized.

—Address to XXI Plenary Assembly of the Pontifical Council for the Family, October 2013

These children are a link in a chain. . . . Such is the chain of faith! What does this mean? I would like to tell you only this: you are those who transmit the faith, the transmitters; you have a duty to hand on the faith to these children. It is the most beautiful inheritance you will leave to them: the faith! Only this. Today, take this thought home with you. We must be transmitters of the faith. Think about this, always think about how to hand on the faith to your children.

—Homily Feast of the Baptism of the Lord and at the administration of baptism, Sistine Chapel, January 12, 2014

No elderly person should be like an "exile" in our families. The elderly are a treasure for our society.

—Tweet, January 11, 2014

In the Our Father prayer we say, "Give us this day our daily bread." Married couples may also learn to pray, "Give us this day our daily love," teach us to love each other, to care for each other. The more you entrust yourselves to the Lord, the more your love will be "for ever," able to renew itself and to overcome every difficulty.

—Address to 10,000 engaged couples in St. Peter's Square, February 14, 2014

Today, there are those who say that marriage is out of fashion. Is it out of fashion? In a culture of relativism and the ephemeral. . . . I ask you to swim against the tide; yes, I am asking you to rebel against this culture that sees everything as temporary and that ultimately believes you are incapable of responsibility, that believes you are incapable of true love. I have confidence in you and I pray for you. Have the courage to "swim against the tide." And also have the courage to be happy.

—Address to World Youth Day volunteers, July 28, 2013

The perfect family doesn't exist, nor is there a perfect husband or a perfect wife, and let's not talk about the perfect mother-in-law! It's just us sinners. A healthy family life requires frequent use of three phrases: May I? Thank you, and I'm sorry and never, never, never end the day without making peace.

—Address to 10,000 engaged couples in St. Peter's Square, February 14, 2014

So many children don't know how to pray!

—Homily, Ash Wednesday 2004

Dear parents, teach your children to pray. Pray with them.

—Tweet, April 1, 2014

There was a priest who said that God made us man and woman so that we would love one another and be needed by one another. In preaching on marriage I usually say to the groom that he has to make the bride more of a woman and to the bride that she has to make the groom more of a man.

—*On Heaven and Earth: Pope Francis on Faith, Family, and the Church in the Twenty-First Century* by Jorge Mario Bergoglio and Abraham Skorka

The "home" represents the most precious human treasures, that of encounter, that of relations among people, different in age, culture and history, but who live together and together help one another to grow. For this reason, the "home" is a crucial place in life, where life grows and can be fulfilled, because it is a place in which every person learns to receive love and to give love.

—Address during visit to homeless shelter, May 21, 2013

A good father, like a good mother, is one who intervenes in the life of his child just enough to demonstrate guidelines for growing up, to help him, but who later knows when to be a bystander to his own and others' failures, and to endure them.

—***Pope Francis: Conversations with Jorge Bergoglio***
edited by Francesca Ambrogetti and Sergio Rubin

Do I, like Mary, remain steadfast? How are your parents? How are your grandparents? How are your in-laws? Are you there for them? Do you care about them? Do you visit them? Sometimes it is very painful but there is no other choice than to put them in a nursing home for health reasons or family situations. But once they are there, do I set aside a Saturday or a Sunday to be with them? Do you care for that life that is fading away and that gave life to you?

—Homily, March 25, 2011

Let us pray for peace, and let us bring it about, starting in our own homes!

—Tweet, January 16, 2014

It means caring for one another in our families: husbands and wives first protect one another, and then, as parents, they care for their children, and children themselves, in time, protect their parents.

—Address, March 19, 2013

SIN AND FORGIVENESS

I am a sinner. This is the most accurate definition. It is not a figure of speech, a literary genre. I am a sinner.

—Interview with Antonio Spadaro, S.J., editor-in-chief of *La Civiltà Cattolica*, August–September 2013

For me, sin is not a stain that I have to clean. What I should do is ask pardon and make reconciliation, not stop by the cleaner's on my way home.

—*El Jesuita*, 2010

What hurts me the most are the many occasions when I have not been more understanding and impartial. In morning prayers, in supplications, I first ask to be understanding and impartial. I then continue asking for many more things related to my failings as I travel through life. I want to travel with humility, with interpretative goodness. But I must emphasize, I was always loved by God. He lifted me up when I fell along the way.

—*Pope Francis: Conversations with Jorge Bergoglio* edited by Francesca Ambrogetti and Sergio Rubin

Only we big sinners have this grace of knowing what salvation really means.

—*El Jesuita*, 2010

However, there is one problem that can afflict Christians: the spirit of the world, the worldly spirit, spiritual worldliness. This leads to self-sufficiency, to living by the spirit of the world rather than by the spirit of Jesus.

—Address, Pentecost vigil with ecclesial movements, May 18, 2013

In this globalized world, we have fallen into globalized indifference. We have become used to the suffering of others: it doesn't affect me; it doesn't concern me; it's none of my business!

—Homily, July 8, 2013

Gossip can also kill, because it kills the reputation of the person! It is so terrible to gossip! At first it may seem like a nice thing, even amusing, like enjoying a candy. But in the end, it fills the heart with bitterness, and even poisons us.

—Angelus address, February 16, 2014

That is the first characteristic of a stuffy, neat, and tidy Christian, of a hypocrite, of a Pharisee: always feeling the need to criticize others. Let us ask Jesus now for the grace to open our hearts so that his mercy may enter. Let's say: "Yes, Lord, I am a sinner. I am a sinner because of this and because of that. Come, come and justify me before the Father." So be it!

—Homily, September 24, 2011

God's patience is comfortable and sweet like a summer's night.

—***El Jesuita***, **2010**

We must always be on guard, on guard against deceit, against the seduction of evil.

—Homily, October 11, 2013

Sometimes it may seem as though God does not react to evil, as if he is silent. And yet God has spoken. He has replied, and his answer is the cross of Christ: a word that is love, mercy, forgiveness.

—Address, Good Friday, March 29, 2013

The temptation to set God aside . . . is always at the door, and the experience of sin injures our Christian life, our being children of God. For this reason we must have the courage of faith not to allow ourselves to be guided by the mentality that tells us: "God is not necessary, he is not important for you," and so forth. It is exactly the opposite: only by behaving as children of God without despairing at our shortcomings, at our sins, only by feeling loved by him will our life be new, enlivened by serenity and joy! God is our strength! God is our hope!

—Homily, April 10, 2013

Let us look around: how many wounds are inflicted upon humanity by evil! Wars, violence, economic conflicts that hit the weakest, greed for money, power, corruption, divisions, crimes against human life and against creation.

—Homily, Palm Sunday and World Youth Day, March 24, 2013

In life we all make many mistakes. Let us learn to recognize our errors and ask forgiveness.

—Tweet, March 4, 2014

Dear brothers and sisters, let us not be closed to the newness that God wants to bring into our lives! Are we often weary, disheartened, and sad? Do we feel weighed down by our sins? Do we think that we won't be able to cope? Let us not close our hearts; let us not lose confidence; let us never give up. There are no situations which God cannot change; there is no sin which he cannot forgive if only we open ourselves to him.

—Homily, Easter vigil, Holy Saturday, March 30, 2013

Jesus heals our sins. And along the way Jesus comes and forgives us—all of us sinners, we are all sinners—even when we make a mistake, when we commit a sin, when we sin. And this forgiveness that we receive in Confession is an encounter with Jesus.

—Address to parish of Saint Cyril of Alexandria in Rome, December 1, 2013

Let us . . . remember Peter: three times he denied Jesus, precisely when he should have been closest to him; and when he hits bottom he meets the gaze of Jesus who patiently, wordlessly, says to him: "Peter, don't be afraid of your weakness, trust in Me." Peter understands, he feels the loving gaze of Jesus and he weeps. How beautiful is this gaze of Jesus—how much tenderness is there! Brothers and sisters, let us never lose trust in the patience and mercy of God!

—Homily, Divine Mercy Sunday, April 7, 2013

When Jesus stepped into the waters of the Jordan and was baptized by John the Baptist, He did so not because He was in need of repentance, or conversion; He did it to be among people who need forgiveness, among us sinners, and to take upon Himself the burden of our sins. In this way He chose to comfort us, to save us, to free us from our misery.

—Lenten message 2014

Jesus' attitude is striking: we do not hear the words of scorn, we do not hear words of condemnation, but only words of love, of mercy, which are an invitation to conversation. "Neither do I condemn you; go, and do not sin again." Ah! Brothers and Sisters, God's face is the face of a merciful father who is always patient. Have you thought about God's patience, the patience He has with each one of us? That is His mercy.

—Angelus address, March 17, 2013

When was the last time you went to confession? . . . And if a lot of time has passed, don't lose a day! Go ahead, the priest will be good! Jesus is there, right? And Jesus is better than the priest, it is Jesus who receives you. He receives you with great love. Be courageous, and go to Confession!

—General audience, February 19, 2014

If we—all of us—accept the grace of Jesus Christ, he changes our heart and from sinners makes us saints. To become holy, we do not need to turn our eyes away and look somewhere else, or have, as it were, the face on a holy card! No, no, that is not necessary. To become saints, only one thing is necessary: to accept the grace which the Father gives us in Jesus Christ.

—Address, June 17, 2013

THE EQUALITY OF HUMAN BEINGS

No one is the most important person in the Church; we are all equal in God's eyes. Some of you might say, "Listen, Mr. Pope, you are not our equal." Yes, I am like each one of you; we are all equal, we are brothers and sisters!

—General audience, June 26, 2013

Human life, the person is no longer perceived as a primary value to be respected and protected, especially if poor or disabled, if not yet useful—such as the unborn child—or no longer needed—such as the elderly.

—Meeting with Catholic charitable organizations, June 5, 2013

The Church proposes ways of salvation and takes care of society's "leftovers." This is what Jesus did, and this is what we want to do as his disciples and his missionaries. We want to show society, in an open dialogue that includes justice and truth, that the elderly among us are worthy of respect and not pity, that we are indebted to them, and that we owe them esteem and respect, and not merely concern.

—Speech, February 2, 2008

All life has inestimable value even the weakest and most vulnerable, the sick, the old, the unborn and the poor, are masterpieces of God's creation, made in his own image, destined to live forever, and deserving of the utmost reverence and respect.

—Message to Catholics taking part in annual Day for Life in Great Britain and Ireland, July 28, 2013

If [gay people] accept the Lord and have goodwill, who am I to judge them?

—Interview with journalists aboard papal plane, July 29, 2013

Every unborn child, though unjustly condemned to be aborted, has the face of the Lord, who even before his birth, and then as soon as he was born, experienced the rejection of the world. And every old person, even if infirm and at the end of his days, carries with him the face of Christ. They must not be thrown away!

—Address to group of Catholic health-care professionals and gynecologists, September 20, 2013

Abortion is never a solution. We listen, support and [offer] understanding from our place to save two lives: respect the human being small and helpless, they can take steps to preserve your life, allow birth, and then be creative in the search for ways to bring it to its full development.

—Statement in response to Argentina Supreme Court decision to allow abortion in case or threat to a woman's life, 2012

A person once asked me, in a provocative manner, if I approved of homosexuality. I replied with another question: "Tell me: when God looks at a gay person, does he endorse the existence of this person with love, or reject and condemn this person?" We must always consider the person.

—Interview with Antonio Spadaro, S.J., editor-in-chief of *La Civiltà Cattolica*, August–September 2013

THE CHURCH

I see the church as a field hospital after battle. It is useless to ask a seriously injured person if he has high cholesterol and about the level of his blood sugars! You have to heal his wounds. Then we can talk about everything else. Heal the wounds, heal the wounds. And you have to start from the ground up.

—Interview with Antonio Spadaro, S.J., editor-in-chief of *La Civiltà Cattolica*, August–September 2013

We need a Church unafraid of going forth into their night. We need a Church capable of meeting them on their way. We need a Church capable of entering into their conversation. We need a Church able to dialogue with those disciples who, having left Jerusalem behind, are wandering aimlessly, alone, with their own disappointment, disillusioned by a Christianity now considered barren, fruitless soil, incapable of generating meaning.

—Address to the bishops of Brazil, July 27, 2013

In the history of the Catholic Church the true reformers are the saints. They are the true reformers, those that change, transform, carry forward and resurrect the spiritual path. . . . Francis of Assisi contributed an entire concept about poverty to Christianity in the face of the wealth, pride and vanity of the civil and ecclesial powers of the time. He carried out a mysticism of poverty, of dispossession and he has changed history.

—*On Heaven and Earth: Pope Francis on Faith, Family, and the Church in the Twenty-First Century* by Jorge Mario Bergoglio and Abraham Skorka

We need to avoid the spiritual sickness of a Church that is wrapped up in its own world: when a Church becomes like this, it grows sick. It is true that going out onto the street implies the risk of accidents happening, as they would to any ordinary man or woman. But if the Church stays wrapped up in itself, it will age. And if I had to choose between a wounded Church that goes out onto the streets and a sick withdrawn Church, I would definitely choose the first one.

—Interview with *Vatican Insider*, February 2012

We cannot insist only on issues related to abortion, gay marriage and the use of contraceptive methods. This is not possible. I have not spoken much about these things, and I was reprimanded for that. . . . The teaching of the church, for that matter, is clear and I am a son of the church, but it is not necessary to talk about these issues all the time.

—Interview with Antonio Spadaro, S.J., editor-in-chief of *La Civiltà Cattolica*, August–September 2013

We have to pray, together as Catholics and also with other Christians, pray that the Lord give us the gift of unity, unity among us. But how will we have unity among Christians if we are not capable of it among ourselves, as Catholics? Or in our families? So many families fight and are divided! Seek unity, the unity that builds the Church. Unity comes from Jesus Christ. He sends us the Holy Spirit to create unity.

—General audience, June 19, 2013

Look at the Church, holy and sinful as it is; look at certain shortcomings and sins, without losing sight of the holiness of so many men and women who work in the Church today.

—Interview with *Vatican Insider*, February 24, 2012

Despite the slowness, the infidelity, the errors and sins it committed and might still commit against its members, the Church, trust me, has no other meaning and goal but to live and witness Jesus.

—Letter to *La Repubblica*, September 11, 2013

I feel compelled to take personal responsibility for all the evil that some priests, many—many in number, (although) not in comparison with the totality—to assume personal responsibility and to ask forgiveness for the damage caused by the sexual abuse of the children. The church is aware of this damage. We don't want to take a step back in dealing with this problem and the sanctions that must be imposed. On the contrary, I think we must be even stronger! You don't play around with the lives of children.

—Comments to members of the International Catholic Child Bureau, April 2014

Heads of the Church have often been narcissists, flattered and thrilled by their courtiers. The court is the leprosy of the papacy.

—Interview with *La Repubblica* founder, Eugenio Scalfari, October 1, 2013

Let us never yield to pessimism or discouragement: let us be quite certain that the Holy Spirit bestows upon the Church, with his powerful breath, the courage to persevere.

—Address to the cardinals, March 15, 2013

But in justice, I must say first that the contribution of the Church in today's world is enormous. The pain and the shame we feel at the sins of some members of the Church, and at our own, must never make us forget how many Christians are giving their lives in love.

—*The Joy of the Gospel: Apostolic Exhortation*, 2013

The Church is not a charitable, cultural or political association, but a living Body, that walks and acts in history. And this Body has a head, Jesus, who guides, nourishes and supports it.

—General audience, June 19, 2013

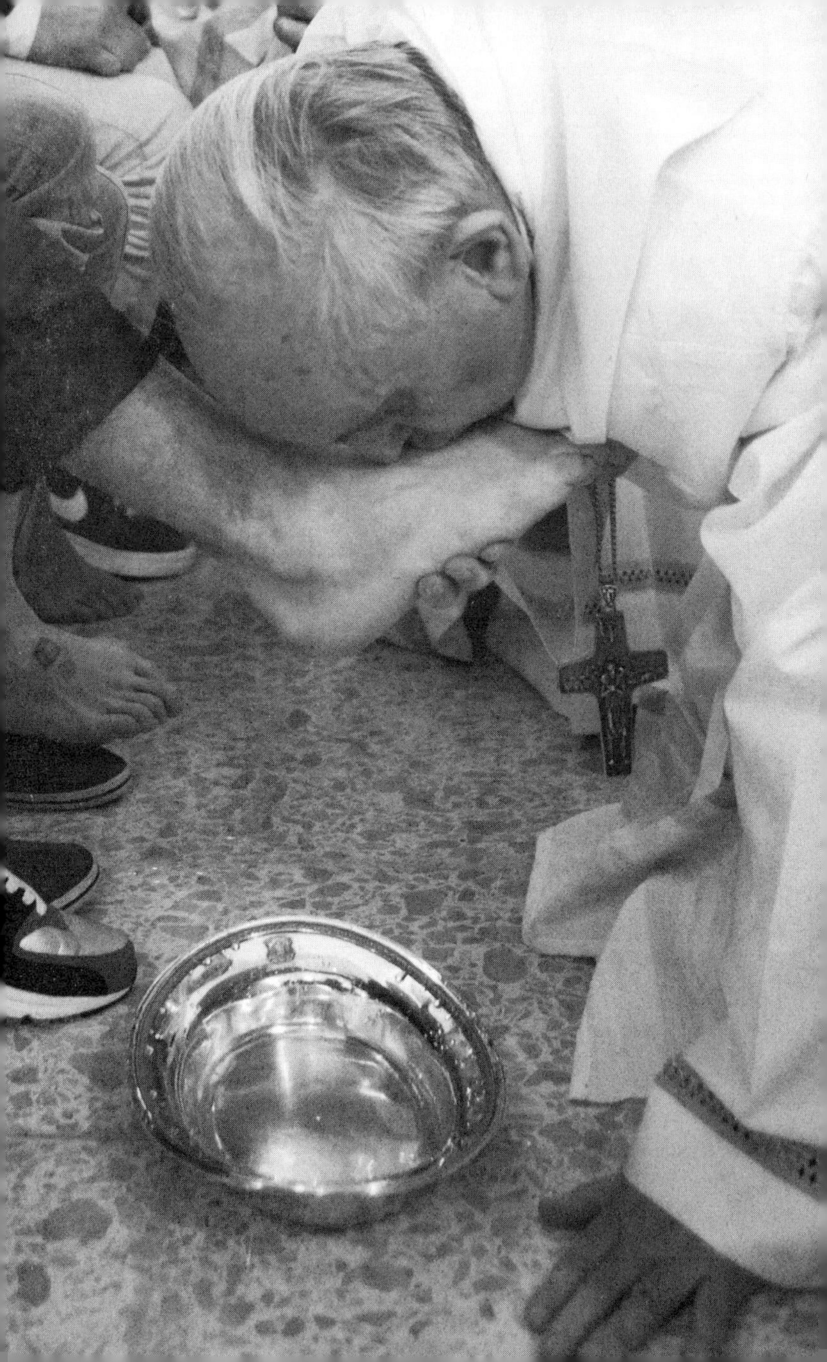

SUFFERING

To suffer is to take the difficulty and to carry it with strength, so that the difficulty does not drag us down. To carry it with strength: this is a Christian virtue.

—Homily, May 24, 2013

In the Cross we see the monstrosity of man, when we allow ourselves to be guided by evil; but we also see the immensity of God's mercy who does not treat us according to our sins, but according to His mercy.

—Way of the Cross address at the Colosseum, April 17, 2014

When we journey without the Cross, when we build without the Cross, when we profess Christ without the Cross, we are not disciples of the Lord, we are worldly: we may be bishops, priests, cardinals, popes, but not disciples of the Lord.

—Homily, March 14, 2013

You might say, "Can't we have a more human Christianity, without the cross, without Jesus, without stripping ourselves?" In this way we'd become pastry-shop Christians, like a pretty cake and nice sweet things. Pretty, but not true Christians.

—In Assisi, October 4, 2013

It is from pain and our own limits where we best learn to grow, and from our own flaws surges the deep question: haven't we suffered enough to decide to break old patterns?

—Homily, May 25, 2002

Christians know that suffering cannot be eliminated, yet it can have meaning and become an act of love and entrustment into the hands of God who does not abandon us; in this way it can serve as a moment of growth in faith and love.

—*Lumen Fidei*, 2013

And the Lord invites us to this: to be rejuvenated Easter people on a journey of love, patience, enduring our tribulations and also—I would say—putting up with one another. We must also do this with charity and love, because if I have to put up with you, I'm sure you will put up with me; and in this way, we will move forward on our journey on the path of Jesus.

—Homily, May 7, 2013

The Son of God made man has not taken away from human disease and suffering, but, taking them upon himself, has transformed and reduced them so they no longer have the last word, which now belongs to the new life in fullness; transformed, because in union with Christ positive can come from negative.

—Message for World Day of the Sick, February 11, 2014

Although the life of a person is in a land full of thorns and weeds, there is always a space in which the good seed can grow. You have to trust God.

—Interview with Antonio Spadaro, S.J., editor-in-chief of *La Civiltà Cattolica*, August–September 2013

PEACE

True peace grows out of the tension between two contrary elements: the acceptance of a present in which we recognize our weakness as sinners, and, at the same time, passing beyond the same present as if we were already freed from the burden of sin.

—*The Joy of the Gospel: Apostolic Exhortation*, 2013

Francis of Assisi tells us we should work to build peace. But there is no true peace without truth! There cannot be true peace if everyone is his own criterion, if everyone can always claim exclusively his own rights, without at the same time caring for the good of others, of everyone, on the basis of the nature that unites every human being on this earth.

—Address, March 22, 2013

Today, dear brothers and sisters, I wish to add my voice to the cry which rises up with increasing anguish from every part of the world, from every people, from the heart of each person, from the one great family which is humanity: it is the cry for peace! It is a cry which declares with force: we want a peaceful world, we want to be men and women of peace, and we want in our society, torn apart by divisions and conflict, that peace break out! War never again! Never again war!

—Angelus address, September 1, 2013

Fighting poverty, both material and spiritual, building peace and constructing bridges: these, as it were, are the reference points for a journey that I want to invite each of the countries here represented to take up. But it is a difficult journey, if we do not learn to grow in love for this world of ours.

—Address to the diplomatic corps accredited by the Holy See, March 22, 2013

Wars shatter so many lives. I think especially of children robbed of their childhood.

—Tweet, January 18, 2014

This morning I celebrated Holy Mass with several soldiers and with the parents of some of those who died in the missions for peace, who seek to further reconciliation and peace in countries in which so much fraternal blood is spilled in wars that are always madness. "Everything is lost in war. Everything is gained with peace."

—Angelus address, June 2, 2013

On the Cross Jesus knocked down the wall of enmitythat divides people and nations, and he brought reconciliation and peace.

—Homily, Palm Sunday and World Youth Day, March 24, 2013

My Christian faith urges me to look to the Cross. How I wish that all men and women of good will would look to the Cross if only for a moment! There, we can see God's reply: violence is not answered with violence, death is not answered with the language of death. In the silence of the Cross, the uproar of weapons ceases and the language of reconciliation, forgiveness, dialogue, and peace is spoken.

—Address, prayer vigil for peace, September 7, 2013

Peace to the whole world, torn apart by violence linked to drug trafficking and by the iniquitous exploitation of natural resources! Peace to this our Earth! May the risen Jesus bring comfort to the victims of natural disasters and make us responsible guardians of creation.

—Easter Sunday message, March 31, 2013

THE BLESSED MOTHER

Our Lady is always close to us, especially when we feel the weight of life with all its problems.

—Tweet, February 24, 2014

In her Canticle, Mary does not say she is happy because God was looking to her virginity, to her kindness or to her sweetness—all of them virtues that she possessed. . . . No, because the Lord was looking to her humility, the humility of His servant, her smallness.

—Homily, March 24, 2014

Let us invoke the intercession of Mary who is the Woman of the "yes." Mary said "yes" throughout her life! She learned to recognize Jesus' voice from the time when she carried him in her womb. May Mary, our Mother, help us to know Jesus' voice better and better and to follow it, so as to walk on the path of life!

—Homily, April 21, 2013

Mary was able to turn a stable into a home for Jesus, with poor swaddling clothes and an abundance of love. She is the handmaid of the Father who sings his praises. She is the friend who is ever concerned that wine not be lacking in our lives. She is the woman whose heart was pierced by a sword and who understands all our pain.

—*The Joy of the Gospel: Apostolic Exhortation*, 2013

Mary was an expert in listening.

—Homily, August 7, 2006

Our gratitude must be like Mary's, who, in spite of all the sorrows she had to endure, did not cast down her eyes in defeat, but instead sang of the greatness of the Lord.

—Lenten letter, February 22, 2012

The Mother of the Redeemer goes before us and continually strengthens us in faith, in our vocation and in our mission. By her example of humility and openness to God's will she helps us to transmit our faith in a joyful proclamation of the Gospel to all, without reservation. In this way our mission will be fruitful, because it is modeled on the motherhood of Mary. To her let us entrust our journey of faith, the desires of our heart, our needs and the needs of the whole world, especially of those who hunger and thirst for justice and peace, and for God.

—Homily, Feast of the Solemnity of Mary, Mother of God, January 1, 2014

May the Virgin Mary, our Mother, who is the beloved model both of God and his people in listening to and imparting messages of good news, receive our prayers and grant us the grace of knowing how to listen.

—Homily, August 7, 2006

With the Holy Spirit, Mary is always present in the midst of the people. She joined the disciples in praying for the coming of the Holy Spirit (Acts 1:14) and thus made possible the missionary outburst which took place at Pentecost. She is the Mother of the Church which evangelizes, and without her we could never truly understand the spirit of the new evangelization.

—***The Joy of the Gospel: Apostolic Exhortation*, 2013**

I commit my ministry, and your ministry, to the powerful intercession of Mary, our Mother, Mother of the Church. Beneath her maternal gaze, may each one of us walk and listen to the voice of her divine Son, strengthening unity, persevering together in prayer, and giving witness to the true faith in the continual presence of the Lord.

—Address to the College of Cardinals, March 15, 2013

WOMEN

The first witnesses of the Resurrection were women. And this is beautiful. This is part of the mission of women; of mothers, of women! Witnessing to their children, to their grandchildren, that Jesus is alive, is living, is risen. Mothers and women, carry on witnessing to this! It is the heart that counts for God, how open to him we are, whether we are like trusting children.

—Address, April 3, 2013

I congratulate you on seeing that many women share pastoral responsibilities with priests, helping to guide people, families and groups and offering new contributions to theological reflection. Indeed, I hoped that increasing space may be offered to women for a more widespread and incisive presence in the Church.

—Address to the National Congress of the Italian Women's Centre, January 25, 2014

These new opportunities and responsibilities which have opened, and which I sincerely hope may further expand by the presence and work of women, both within the ecclesial and civil and professional spheres, cannot make us forget the woman's irreplaceable role in the family. The gifts of refinement, particular sensitivity and tenderness, with which the woman's spirit is richly endowed, represent not only a genuine strength for the life of the family, for spreading a climate of serenity and harmony, but a reality without which the human vocation cannot be fulfilled.

—Address to the National Congress of the Italian Women's Centre, January 25, 2014

In the theologically grounded tradition the priesthood passes through man. The woman has another function in Christianity, reflected in the figure of Mary. It is the figure that embraces society, the figure that contains it, the mother of the community. The woman has the gift of maternity, of tenderness; if all these riches are not integrated, a religious community not only transforms into a chauvinist society, but also into one that is austere, hard and hardly sacred. The fact that a woman cannot exercise the priesthood does not make her less than the male.

—*On Heaven and Earth: Pope Francis on Faith, Family, and the Church in the Twenty-First Century* by Jorge Mario Bergoglio and Abraham Skorka

All the mothers and all the grandmothers who are here should think about this: passing on the faith! Because God sets beside us people who help us on our journey of faith. We do not find our faith in the abstract, no! It is always a person preaching who tells us who Jesus is, who communicates faith to us and gives us the first proclamation. And this is how I received my first experience of faith.

—Address, Pentecost vigil with ecclesial movements, May 18, 2013

A church without women would be like the apostolic college without Mary. The Madonna is more important than the apostles, and the church herself is feminine, the spouse of Christ and a mother.

—Addressing journalists on the plane returning to Rome from World Youth Day, July 29, 2013

She [Mary] is the authentic feminine genius. And let us think about Our Lady in families—about what Our Lady does in a family. It is clear that the presence of a woman in the domestic sphere is more necessary than ever, indeed for the transmission of sound moral principles and for the transmission of the faith itself to future generations.

—Address to the National Congress of the Italian Women's Centre, January 25, 2014

Women are asking deep questions that must be addressed. The church cannot be herself without the woman and her role. The woman is essential for the church. Mary, a woman, is more important than the bishops.

—Interview with Antonio Spadaro, S.J., editor-in-chief of *La Civiltà Cattolica*, August–September 2013

RELIGION

The word religion precisely means to come to assume a bond with the Lord by means of searching. If a religion is purely ritualistic, without this type of content, it is destined to die because it fills you with rites but it leaves the heart empty.

—On Heaven and Earth: Pope Francis on Faith, Family, and the Church in the Twenty-First Century
by Jorge Mario Bergoglio and Abraham Skorka

In this, we also sense our closeness to all those men and women who, although not identifying themselves as followers of any religious tradition, are nonetheless searching for truth, goodness and beauty, the truth, goodness and beauty of God. They are our valued allies in the commitment to defending human dignity, in building a peaceful coexistence between peoples and in safeguarding and caring for creation.

—Address to representatives of the churches, ecclesial communities, and different religions, March 20, 2013

Jesus does not force you to be a Christian. But if you say you are a Christian, you must believe that Jesus has all power—and is the only one who has the power—to renew the world, to renew your life, to renew your family, to renew the community, to renew all things. This is the message that we need to take away with us today, asking the Father to help us to be docile to the promptings of the Spirit who does this work, the Spirit of Jesus.

—Homily, February 18, 2012

That is the religious experience: the astonishment of meeting someone who is waiting for you.

—***El Jesuita***, **2010**

Not everyone present belongs to the Catholic faith, and others do not believe. I respect the conscience of each one of you, knowing that each one of you is a child of God. May God bless you.

—Vatican press conference, March 16, 2013

Dialogue and friendship with the children of Israel are part of the life of Jesus' disciples. The friendship which has grown between us makes us bitterly and sincerely regret the terrible persecutions which they have endured, and continue to endure, especially those that have involved Christians.

—***The Joy of the Gospel: Apostolic Exhortation***, **2013**

Faced with disconcerting episodes of violent fundamentalism, our respect for true followers of Islam should lead us to avoid hateful generalizations, for authentic Islam and the proper reading of the Koran are opposed to every form of violence.

—***The Joy of the Gospel: Apostolic Exhortation***, **2013**

I am respectful of all new spiritual proposals, but they must be authentic and submit themselves to the passage of time, which will reveal if their message is temporary or will live on through the generations. Surviving the passage of time is the major test of spiritual purity.

—*On Heaven and Earth: Pope Francis on Faith, Family, and the Church in the Twenty-First Century* by Jorge Mario Bergoglio and Abraham Skorka

We Christians bring peace and grace as a treasure to be offered to the world, but these gifts can bear fruit only when Christians live and work together in harmony. This makes it easier to contribute to building relations of respect and peaceful coexistence with those who belong to other religious traditions, and with non-believers.

—Address to the Archbishop of Canterbury, June 14, 2013

THE MODERN WORLD

The culture of selfishness and individualism that often prevails in our society is not, I repeat, not what builds up and leads to a more habitable world: rather, it is the culture of solidarity that does so; the culture of solidarity means seeing others not as rivals or statistics, but brothers and sisters.

—Address, World Youth Day, July 25, 2013

When we do not profess Jesus Christ, we profess the worldliness of the devil, a demonic worldliness.

—Homily, March 14, 2013

The speed with which information is communicated exceeds our capacity for reflection and judgment, and this does not make for more balanced and proper forms of self-expression. . . . The world of communications can help us either to expand our knowledge or to lose our bearings. The desire for digital connectivity can have the effect of isolating us from our neighbors, from those closest to us. We should not overlook the fact that those who for whatever reason lack access to social media run the risk of being left behind.

—Message for the 48th World Communications Day, January 24, 2014

We live in a society that leaves no room for God; day by day this numbs our hearts.

—Tweet, March 29, 2014

Certainly, possessions, money, and power can give a momentary thrill, the illusion of being happy, but they end up possessing us and making us always want to have more, never satisfied. . . . "Put on Christ" in your life, place your trust in him and you will never be disappointed!

—Address, World Youth Day, July 25, 2013

Young people at the moment are in crisis. We have all become accustomed to this disposable culture. We do the same thing with the elderly, but with all these people out of work even they are afflicted by a culture where everything is disposable. We have to stop this habit of throwing things away. We need a culture of inclusion.

—Addressing journalists on the plane returning to Rome from World Youth Day, July 2013

The world makes us look towards ourselves, our possessions, our desires. The Gospel invites us to be open to others, to share with the poor.

—Tweet, February 6, 2014

We have, in our hands, the responsibility and also the possibility of making this world much better for our children.

—Homily, Easter 2005

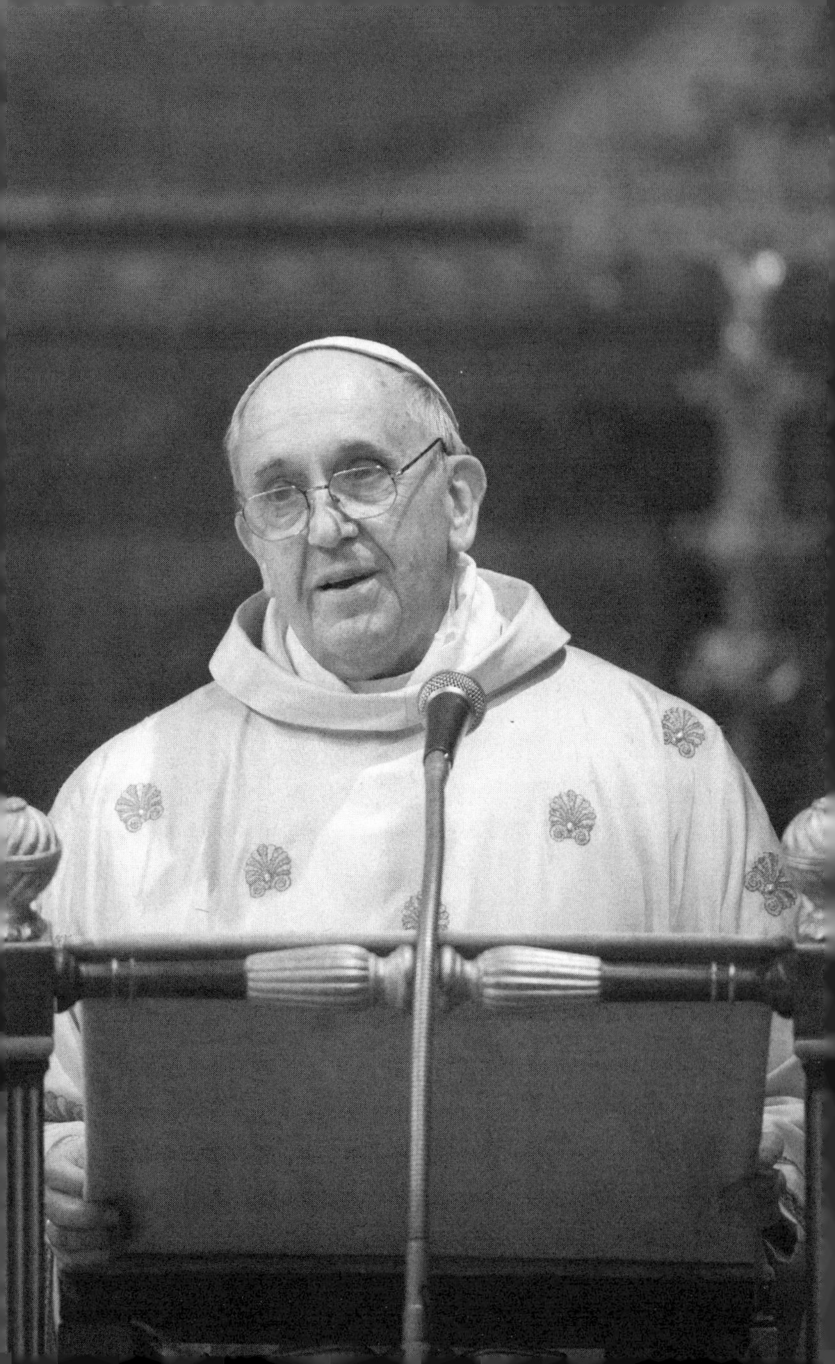

THE WISDOM OF POPE FRANCIS

We have just listened to the Passion of our Lord. We might well ask ourselves just one question: Who am I? Who am I, before my Lord? Who am I, before Jesus who enters Jerusalem amid the enthusiasm of the crowd? Am I ready to express my joy, to praise him? Or do I stand back? Who am I, before the suffering Jesus?

—Homily, Palm Sunday and World Youth Day, April 13, 2014

We too should be clear in our Christian life that entering the glory of God demands daily fidelity to his will, even when it demands sacrifice and sometimes requires us to change our plans.

—General audience, April 17, 2014

We are all simple but important instruments of his; we have not received the gift of faith to keep it hidden, but, rather, to spread it so that it can illumine a great many of our brethren on their journey.

—Address to meeting of the Pontifical Mission Societies, May 17, 2013

This evening I would like a question to resound in the heart of each one of you, and I would like you to answer it honestly: Have I considered which idol lies hidden in my life that prevents me from worshiping the Lord? Worshiping is stripping ourselves of our idols, even the most hidden ones, and choosing the Lord as the center, as the highway of our lives.

—Homily, April 14, 2013

How good it is for us when the Lord unsettles our lukewarm and superficial lives.

—**Tweet, April 7, 2014**

Listening is not simply hearing. Listening is being attentive. Listening is the desire to understand, to value, to respect, and to save. We must find the means to listen attentively so that each person may speak and so that we are aware of what each person wishes to say.

—**Homily, August 7, 2006**

The commandments are not a litany of prohibitions—you must not do this, you must not do that, you must not do the other; on the contrary, they are a great "Yes!": a yes to God, to Love, to life.

—**Homily, June 16, 2013**

What does freedom mean? It is certainly not doing whatever you want, allowing yourself to be dominated by the passions, to pass from one experience to another without discernment, to follow the fashions of the day; freedom does not mean, so to speak, throwing everything that you don't like out the window. . . . Let us not be afraid of life commitments, commitments that take up and concern our entire life! In this way our life will be fruitful! And this is freedom: to have the courage to make these decisions with generosity.

—**Address, May 4, 2013**

I am always wary of decisions made hastily. I am always wary of the first decision, that is, the first thing that comes to my mind if I have to make a decision. This is usually the wrong thing. I have to wait and assess, looking deep into myself, taking the necessary time.

—Homily, August 7, 2006

The life of slumbering Christians is a sad life, it is not a happy life. Christians must be happy, with the joy of Jesus. Let us not fall asleep!

—Homily, April 24, 2013

The Gospel is very clear: we need to go back there, to see Jesus risen, and to become witnesses of his resurrection. This is not to go back in time; it is not a kind of nostalgia. It is returning to our first love, in order to receive the fire which Jesus has kindled in the world and to bring that fire to all people, to the very ends of the earth.

—Homily, Easter vigil, Holy Saturday, April 19, 2014

Say yes to closeness, to walking with God's people. Say yes to tenderness, especially toward sinners and toward outcasts, knowing that God dwells among them.

—Homily, September 2, 2012

Do not be afraid, because the Lord is the Lord of consolation, he is the Lord of tenderness. The Lord is a Father, and he says that he will be for us like a mother with her baby, with a mother's tenderness. Do not be afraid of the consolations of the Lord.

—Homily, June 29, 2013

Grace is not part of consciousness; it is the amount of light in our souls, not knowledge nor reason.

—General audience, September 25, 2013

Let us too have greater courage in witnessing to our faith in the Risen Christ! We must not be afraid of being Christian and living as Christians! We must have this courage to go and proclaim the Risen Christ, for he is our peace, he made peace with his love, with his forgiveness, with his Blood, and with his mercy.

—Homily, Divine Mercy Sunday, April 7, 2013

This is the invitation which I address to everyone: Let us accept the grace of Christ's resurrection! Let us be renewed by God's mercy; let us be loved by Jesus; let us enable the power of his love to transform our lives, too; and let us become agents of this mercy, channels through which God can water the earth, protect all creation and make justice and peace flourish.

—Easter Sunday message, March 31, 2013

RECOLLECTIONS OF POPE FRANCIS

There was a lot of joy for many reasons . . . most importantly, because what you see with him is what he is. There's no radical difference between Jorge before and Francis after, he's the same person. Now that he is pope, he continues to be himself, and God does the rest.

—Father Fernando Cervera, S.J., now fifty years old, a former student and spiritual advisee of Father Bergoglio, from *Pope Francis: Our Brother, Our Friend* edited by Alejandro Bermúdez, 2013

He emphasizes concern for people, for the person. Bergoglio has never had an abstract concern; he always is concerned about the concrete person, the victim of injustices or poverty. As a priest and a bishop, he went through many neighborhoods in Buenos Aires where he always knew people by name, and, because of this, people love him a lot.

—Bishop Hugo Salaberry, S.J., bishop of Azul, Argentina, from *Pope Francis: Our Brother, Our Friend* edited by Alejandro Bermúdez, 2013

As Pope, Francis has simplified the Renaissance regalia of the papacy by abandoning fur-trimmed velvet capes, choosing to live in a two-room apartment instead of the Apostolic Palace, and replacing the papal Mercedes with a Ford Focus. Instead of the traditional red slip-ons, Francis wears ordinary black shoes.

—James Carroll, "Who Am I to Judge?: A Radical Pope's First Year" *The New Yorker*, December 23, 2013

It was my birthday, and the pope called to wish me a happy birthday just as he's called me now for many years. He remembers our birthday, mine and that of my twin brother, because since he was the provincial, he was the one who admitted us to the Society of Jesus. . . . He had that kind of sensibility, but he surprised me when he called me now as the pope.

—Brother Mario Rafael Rausch, S.J., sixty-year-old Jesuit brother, from *Pope Francis: Our Brother, Our Friend* edited by Alejandro Bermúdez, 2013

I couldn't believe it. We laughed and joked for eight minutes. It was certainly the best day of my life.

—Stefano Cabizza, an IT student from Padua who wrote to Pope Francis and received a phone call in response from the pontiff. The young man was dumbstruck when he answered the phone to hear, "This is Pope Francis," on the other end. As reported in *The Guardian*, August 22, 2013

To understand Pope Francis it is first of all necessary to know the importance he places on mission. The Church exists to continue the healing and saving ministry of Christ. And so Pope Francis reaches out to the poor and marginalized and brings them to the center of the Church's life—just as Christ did so many years ago.

—Father Larry Snyder, president of Catholic Charities USA, USCCBLOG, March 11, 2014

Rarely has a new player on the world stage captured so much attention so quickly—young and old, faithful and cynical—as has Pope Francis. In his nine months in office, he has placed himself at the very center of the central conversations of our time: about wealth and poverty, fairness and justice, transparency, modernity, globalization, the role of women, the nature of marriage, the temptations of power.

—Nancy Gibbs, managing editor of *Time* magazine, on the choice of Pope Francis as 2013 Person of the Year

"Who am I to judge?" That was his answer when asked about homosexuality by a reporter in July. Many assumed Francis, with those words, was changing church doctrine. Instead, he was merely changing its tone, searching for a pragmatic path to reach the faithful who had been repelled by their church or its emphasis on strict dos and don'ts. . . . He is urging his army to think more broadly.

—Howard Chua-Eoan and Elizabeth Dias, "Pope Francis, The People's Pope," *Time* magazine, December 23, 2013

I think Pope Francis is showing himself to be just an extraordinarily thoughtful and soulful messenger of peace and justice.

—Barack Obama, interview with MSNBC, December 2013

He is pastor-in-chief for the world and his major theme is mercy.

—Sister Mary Ann Walsh, spokeswoman for the U.S. Conference of Catholic Bishops

He's captured the world's imagination. Like Jesus, he's always saying, hate the sin, love the sinner. Truth and love have always got to be balanced, and I think he's doing that brilliantly.

—Cardinal Timothy Dolan, head of the U.S. Conference of Catholic Bishops

He is not a showman in the way John Paul was, and he's not retiring in the way Benedict was. Francis is completely comfortable in his own skin. He is transparently a happy person . . . It sounds really simplistic, but unfeigned happiness on the part of a public figure is not that common.

—Father John Wauck, Professor at the Opus Dei Pontifical University of the Holy Cross in Rome, from "One Year Later, 'A Pope for All' Keeps Catholics Guessing," by Sylvia Poggioli, NPR News, March 13, 2014

As a priest, he has positively challenged my brother priests and me with his simple lifestyle, his obvious servant leadership, his reminders about what is most important in our priestly ministry and his contagious joyful spirit. Pope Francis has provided new energy and focus for many priests.

—Archbishop Joseph E. Kurtz, archbishop of Louisville, Kentucky, and president of the U.S. Conference of Catholic Bishops, USCCBLOG, March 10, 2014

If the Church becomes like him and becomes what he wants it to be, it will be an epochal change.

—Eugenio Scalfari, from "How the Church will Change," *La Repubblica*, October 1, 2013

[Pope Francis's] beacon of hope will bring more light than any advancement of science, because no drug has the power of love.

—Elton John

Rare is the leader who makes us want to be better people. Pope Francis is such a leader.

—Barack Obama, quoted in *Time* magazine's "The 100 Most Influential People," April 23, 2014

CHRONOLOGY

December 17, 1936 — Jorge Mario Bergoglio is born in Buenos Aires, Argentina. He is the son of Mario Jose Bergoglio, who is an Italian immigrant, and Regina Maria (Sivori) Bergoglio, an Argentinean of Italian descent.

1954 — Graduates high school with a diploma in chemical technology.

1957— At the age of 21, becomes seriously ill with pneumonia. As a result, part of his right lung is removed.

March 11, 1958 — Feels called to the priesthood and enters the Society of Jesus as a novice.

March 12, 1960 — Takes first vows as a Jesuit and studies humanities in Padre Hurtado, Chile.

1961 to 1963 — Studies philosophy at San Miguel Seminary in Buenos Aires.

1964 to 1965 — Teaches literature and psychology at a Jesuit secondary school in Santa Fe, Argentina.

1966 — Teaches at Colegio del Salvador secondary school in Buenos Aires.

1967 TO 1970 — Studies theology at Colegio Máximo.

DECEMBER 13, 1969 — Ordained a priest.

1970 TO 1971— Completes "tertianship," or third probation period, in Jesuit formation in Spain.

APRIL 22, 1973 — Takes his final Jesuit vows. From 1973 to 1979 he serves as Jesuit provincial of Argentina and Uruguay.

1979 TO 1985 — Becomes rector and theology instructor at Colegio Máximo.

JUNE 27, 1992 — Father Jorge Bergoglio is appointed as auxiliary bishop in Buenos Aires.

FEBRUARY 28, 1998 — Becomes archbishop of Buenos Aires.

FEBRUARY 21, 2001— Pope John Paul II appoints Bergoglio as a cardinal of the Catholic church.

2005 — Cardinal Bergoglio purportedly receives the second-highest number of votes in conclave that elected Cardinal Joseph Ratzinger to papacy as Pope Benedict XVI after the death of Pope John Paul II.

2005 TO 2011 — Serves as president of Argentine Bishops Conference.

March 13, 2013 — Elected as the 266th pope of the Catholic church after two days and five ballots.

March 23, 2013 — Pope Francis meets Pope Emeritus Benedict, the first time such a meeting has taken place in more than 600 years. Pope Francis is flown by helicopter to Castel Gandolfo for the private lunch with Pope Emeritus Benedict.

March 2013 — Decides not to live in papal apartments but opts instead to reside in Casa Santa Marta, a Vatican guesthouse.

April 2013 — Sets up an advisory board of cardinals gathered from all over the world to assist him in governing the Catholic church.

June 2013 — Establishes a commission to examine Vatican financial institutions.

July 2013 — Presides over 14th International World Youth Day celebration in Rio de Janeiro, Brazil, from July 23rd through July 28th. More than three million people attend.

October 2013 — Visits Assisi, the birthplace of St. Francis. He makes a pilgrimage tracing the steps of St. Francis and is met by thousands of the faithful.

December 2013 — Named 2013 "Person of the Year" by *Time* magazine.

January 2014 — *Rolling Stone* magazine features Pope Francis on its cover.

March 2014 — Creates commission, including an equal number of women and men and more laypeople than clergy, to advise him on sexual abuse policy.

April 27, 2014 — Declares Pope John XXIII and Pope John Paul II saints in the first-ever dual papal canonization.

IMAGE CREDITS

Landov: © Reuters/Landov

Newscom: © ABACA 122; © AFP/Getty Images 98; © Claudia Conteris 80; © Patrick Hertzog: 104; © Romano Osservatore 48; 92, 128; © Reuters 132; © Eric Vandeville 28; © Leonardo Zavattaro 20; © Zuma Press 58, 66, 72

Shutterstock: © giulio napolitano 8, 14, 34, 40, 86, 116; © Martin Podzorny endpapers